REFLECTIONS Of LIFE

Moments of Time from the Heart of a Poet

Phillip Sanchez

Dadielte Production
Moreno Valley, CA
2025

Copyright© 2025 – Phillip Sanchez

Moreno Valley, California

All rights reserved. No part of this book may be reproduced or transmitted in any form or by any means, electronic or mechanical, including photocopying, recording, or by an information storage and retrieval system – except by a reviewer who may quote brief passages in a review to be printed in a magazine, newspaper, or on the Web – without permission in writing from the publisher. For information, please contact Dadielte Production, P.O. Box 1266, Moreno Valley, CA 92556-1266.

ISBN-978-0-9981419-6-1

Published and distributed by

Dadielte Production

Moreno Valley, CA. 92556-1266

First Printing,

Cover design by Marc *Sierre'*

ACKNOWLEDGEMENT

Thank you so very much to the Moreno Valley Scribes for contributing to the expansion of my writing creations and my writing styles.

A special thanks to Anna Christian for her overall guidance and contributions encouraging me to actually go-forward to publish this, my first book.

In addition, a thank you to Debra Anderson, and Mona Stallworth.

To you all

A Big Big Thank You

DEDICATION

To all who seek to share, create and contribute to the Arts and the wellbeing of Humanity. To you, I dedicate this book

Keep on Creating!

TABLE OF CONTENTS

BOOK OF POETRY.

First Poem					Page 7

Last Poem					Page 95

BOOK OF STORIES

First Story					Page 98

Last Story Page				Page 135

Book of Poetry

Today, This day

Today, this day

I turn 78 years of age

I look in the mirror, and I have to look again

Who is that old wrinkled up man, that viejo (Spanish for old man)?

What happened que paso? To you

How very sad, Que lastima (how sad)

Well, aside from the sorry looking sight of me, the image of the very old man of the sea.

I do come to the realization that, yes, I'm 78 now

Many mixed feelings

Don't know why I feel a little melancholy

Memories of my youth and my parents come to my heart now

With it, quite sadness.

Don't know how much longer

My Father will grant me Life

It's unknown

That light at the end of the tunnel grows smaller

And smaller, day by day by day.

But, on the other side of the coin

I'm ever so grateful for

The true blessing of this my Life

A healthy body, mind, and spirit

Comforts and Joys: the thrill of dancing, of attending

and listening to concerts, plays, of catching a huge

yellowfin tuna.

Good times with Loved ones: family and good friends

All these, Given to me by the grace of God.

But, I do have one major correction that needs to

come into being.

I really do need to be much more positive

And, not so critical and judgmental

Sometimes knowledge can be a curse

As passion can also sometimes be.

Hardwired to hate injustice

Regardless of its form, color or shape

So, I tell myself, Phillip, do these few things to maintain

a good and healthy balance

When that passionate anger touches your heart

Take a deep breath, exhale slowly and, take one more breath and just sing the words of one of your favorite songs: Phillip, Here's a few lyrics for you.

"In every life we have some trouble, when you worry you make it double,

Don't Worry, Be Happy."

The referenced song is "Don't Worry, Be Happy" by Bobby McFerrin

Sense Then the Colors of the Wind

Do you feel them

They are ever so subtle

They do touch you

Brushing ever so smoothly

against your skin

It's quiet, its subtle

Yet it is there

Sense then the Colors of the Wind

Do you see it

It is so obvious

It quietly floats through the strong trees

It is so easily seen

It is so Peaceful

It is so Relaxing

Sense the colors of the Wind

The scent of a fresh rose blooming

So fine and pleasing

Sense the Colors of

the Wind

It flows ever so quietly

through

The leaves of the trees

Not a loud and blazing sound

But soft and quiet

It comes upon you

It reminds me of our Connection

With God

With our Creator

Yes, as one with the Universe

With all Life

And all its splendor

Touch me than

Let me sense again

The Colors of the Wind.

For Richard

My Brother,

In a foreign land so far away were you

In that moment

That the bullet entered your body

You must have had so much pain, so much fear

Thoughts, must have flown by in the moment of your

death

You must have felt so desperate and so alone

I was just seven on that terrible day

Oh, how I wish I could have been there

To hold your hand, to comfort you

in those last minutes of your Life

Letting you know Family was there with you

So young were you,

Just 19 years of age

So much Life you lost that day

My Brother Richard, my Brother Richard,

I do say your name

And I carry your flame of Life

Always, in this, my Heart and Soul

RICHARD SANCHEZ
UTAH
PFC 1 MED BN 1 MARINE DIV
KOREA
JAN 1, 1933   MARCH 3, 1952

The Culprit

The Culprit lingers

In the shadows never wanting you to see him

Hiding away from the sunlight of joy and truth

He's an expert, a professional

Ever so good at camouflaging his thirst for

more and more

Much more than he needs

He lives in the realm of gluttony, hoarding and excess

He can shift and move

Ever so quickly depriving so many

Just to take more for himself in the wink of an eye

He's always there, seeking

Seeking that moment

That chance to take the wellbeing, security and

happiness of another

He's clocked seeing the necessity of hiding

Alas, he cannot be seen

He hides in the minds and the flesh

But not in the heart of man

Call him then, Greed.

When will I feel you, my father?

When will I touch your beloved Face?

When will I join with you?

Is it soon, is it soon, my Father?

Only you can tell me

But,

Wait, wait...

I see,

I see something

I think I feel something

Can it be true, is it really happening?

Yes, my Father, yes

It is ....

Really true?

There is no mystery

You are in our lifetime

We only have to look

You are here

I feel you, yes, I can even sense you

So pure, so great, so humble

So obvious

Now at last, I am complete

Thank you, thank you so much

My Great and Heavenly Father.

As Given, by a Believer

In Contemplation

I listen to the sound and the feel of my heart beat

Still so strong, so consistent

In quiet contemplation

Only God knows how much longer it will beat

Reflections of my Life and all the moments I have felt,

seen, touched and experienced (while present here, on

Earth)

Our Life is so strong, yet very much more fragile

We rush through each day

Finding something to do, something to accomplish

Believing that we must fill each and every hour with an

activity

Such a destructive and harmful path

So subtle, yet so demanding

Alas, feel then your heartbeat

Sit quietly, feel your beautiful heartbeat

Hear and feel your breath, hear it, imagine it as it

Fills every organ in your body with the breath of Life

As worrisome thoughts seek to invade your Peace,

see them then

Put them aside and again feel your breath

Such then is the Peace of Mind, Body, and Spirit

Reach for the Stars

Dare to Challenge with your Heart

Fear not, those that hide

In the Security of the Norm

Fight for the Future

of Generations

Only you, only you

Can do this

Don't let the Glitter and the Gold

Fool you

A lot said about the Glitz and the Glamor

Only the Human Heart knows

In it lies the House of God

In Love, so in Love with

His Purity, his Greatness

Touch me, my Father

Love me, my Father

Yours Eternally,

The Cloth

All I have left is this old tattered worn piece of cloth

So very old now

Time has faded its colors

It was on a crash course to oblivion

When I rescued it.

So many years have passed since

It was free in the wind

Now, it is there for me to see always and every day.

It is the only thing left that is the reminder and the

memory

Of a once vibrant life

Of a Family Legacy

Its pattern is undeniable

Its symbol, freedom

Yes, it was the last thing I saw

The last memory I hold

A memory of a time when my beloved Brother Richard

Was buried in a far-away state of Utah

He still lies there

But

I have the cloth now, I will pass it to my daughter Briella

for safe keeping

So sacred, so beloved, so cherished

These Mighty Colors

Always and forever.

Beware the Beast

Here we are, once again

Facing the potential of a second term of hate and

violence

Emanating from it

The Beast only wants to decide, only wants to control

The Beast has no consideration for Human Life

The Beast sways and laughs swaggering from head to

the left and the right

As if he really was a God

The Beast claims to hear God

Claims to feel God

Claims to be doing God's beckoning

Bare caution to the wind

And know who the evil one is for he was masqueraded

as a former president of a powerful Western Nation.

Seeking more power

He comes before us but one more time.

Listen now to the antichrist and his beckoning fooling

and lying

He knows no courage for he himself is a coward

Follow know more, this false one, this Deceiver, this

Antichrist

Lest he take you too to the road of the abyss, to Hell.

You will know him by his works.

He is called out in the Bible

Behold

Lucifer, the Beast

I Close My Eyes

I close my eyes, and I see

Clear beautiful blue skies

Wildlife everywhere, ever so abundant

It really blows my mind away

I close my eyes and I see high flying frigate birds

flying so high

I still hear the call of the sea lions calling to each other

I feel the cool wind on my face

A boat, close friends and a Pongadero

Only fishing poles in our hands

No TVs, cell phones, no techno gimmicks

Just the Sea, the Sky and all of God's gifts.

I marvel at the greatness of it all

One time, one week in this my Life

The memory will always be

there

God's gift – the Sea of Cortez

The Voice, the Voice

The Voice of Martin Luther King

The Voice, the Voice

That Voice that made you stop and listen,

Made you really contemplate what was being stated

Such a strong and passionate voice that touched most who heard it

The feeling, the feeling, the delivery of that voice and the man who owned it

That wavering, passionate, deep feeling voice.

Daring us to stand up with body, soul and mind, to act

In a non-violent manner

Against racism

Against War

Against Injustice

I heard his great voice many times in my youth as a young man of 18, 19 & 20

And, even now in my older years

I know in my Heart there will never be another

Such a giving, loving and inspiring Man

My dear Martin

Your dreams are now mine too, you do live on even

now

In the hearts, minds and spirits of the Merciful and the

Peacemakers.

Do rest in peace my beloved brother.

Hello FB, Google, Amazon, et al

I decided you can no longer share my personal information FOR free.

I want $200 a month plus 30% of your profit you make on my approved sale of my information.

This will begin immediately upon your receipt of my formal certified proof of delivery of my notification to you.

See copy of CA State Law entitled "What's mine is mine" enclosed.

Henceforth: failure to pay will be punishable by Life Imprisonment with no right of Parole.

Yours's Truly

Active Citizen: P. Sanchez

The Fisherman

Went fishing out of H & M Landing yesterday aboard

the "Malihini"

A 75-foot boat

31 anglers were we fishing out of the Coronado Islands.

Strong winds rushing into your face

Smell of the ocean's scent

Ah, the majestic Pacific, how I do love you

Was a day to remember,

The large boat carries memories, once a PT Boat during

WWII

Now re-furbished, she is still running strong

Today, the first day after

Such a sore body, muscle aches from the head to toe

Small cuts on my hands from handling the line of the

reel

Muscles of the back yelling out to me in heavy pain

Balance is one of the keys, yes balance, maintaining balance
Amongst the waves of rocky ocean, swaying up and down with 5ft. swells
Men on board from every walk of life, from a boilermaker to a dentist.
Sharing moments in time
Fishing rod in hand, muscles tense and ready to react, balance is steady
Waiting, waiting for that first bite.
Oh, my Father, how much I do love you, your creation
Given to me in sheer Love
three handsome yellowtails and two bluefin tunas were my catch for the day.

The Clock

The clock keeps ticking, tick tock, tic tock

Counting down the time, the days, the seconds

I will be on this earth

A constant reminder that my days are limited

We don't know when our clocks will stop ticking

Do we?

More and more, I am aware that I am growing much

older

Sadly, when I see a very old person and what time has

done to them

It does make me stop and think,

"You too, Phillip will be there" save a sudden departure

because

Of an accident or physical calamity

Tick tock, tic tock

Can I not stop you, Mr. clock

And freeze the time from ticking?

Preface - I wrote the following poem for a Senator who took a stance against his own party, which resulted in the Senate approving the Affordable Care Act.

A Soldier has Fallen

A Soldier has fallen

Taken by a terrible disease was he

A Soldier has fallen

In the Life that he lived

So hard he fought for Human Dignity and Decency

A Soldier has fallen

Answered his nation's call to serve and protect

A Soldier has fallen

Held so very long and tortured as a prisoner of war

Suffering intense pain and punishment

A Soldier has fallen

Daring to compromise

Putting Compassion, Dignity and Love of Country

Above political partisanship

A Soldier has fallen

A good man, a gentleman, a courageous man, a father

Truth, Dignity, and Decency

Witnessed by his words and his actions

For Love of County

A Soldier has fallen.

For John McCain

Still feeling the power of Hate

Our Nation seems now on the brink

Which way will we go?

Feels like we are actually moving more toward hate and

intolerance

Wondering if I should re-arm myself again

Words really cannot express the concern I have

We seem to be moving backwards

as a Civilized Nation

Is our nation now on the short path

to self-destruction?

I don't know, I don't know

I don't know if we can now get along with each other

Such hatred and evil coming out of the actions of the

Evil One and his Cohorts

Serious cuts, bruises and wounds in the fabric of this,

our beloved nation

I will remain positive even though I know it may be very

hard at times

Knowing that there are those who really, really seek to hurt others to destroy others who seem
To really have no feelings, no empathy for others
Refusing to follow the words of Christ
"For you did it not to the lesser of these, you did it not unto to me."
Matthew, 25 verse 35- 40
Those of us who believe in dignity, love and compassion
Must remain strong and determined
To reach out
Not, with the closed fist of war
But, with the open hand of friendship
Of forgiveness, love and compassion.

The Last Walk

No so long ago

I took a walk with my daughter,

She was just five years old

I held her hand as we both walked together to her school

All smiles, so happy all the time

She enjoyed our walk like always

Little did she know on this day, this would be the last day

I would have the privilege of walking her to school

For on this day, I would be leaving

I would definitely still be in her Life but, not at home all the time

For I decided to leave, what had turned out to be a very bad marriage

The woman I married made so many demands of me

With her constant displays of extreme anger, constantly yelling at me

I held her little hand, enjoying this so very much of this,

our last walk together

It really broke my heart to do so but

I knew it was the right thing to do

I would still be in her life, part of growing up

To become a beautiful bright young lady and woman

A woman can bring peace and confusion

In peace, she puts out the raw fire that builds in yes, his loins

It can grow and grow

And if left alone and untreated

Can confuse his mind, spirit, and actions

Alone, a Man is nothing, just a lonely burning light

That can grow daily

A woman, brings him peace and happiness

A quiet contentment

A place where he can breathe easy in calm and tranquility

It is amazing what she can bring to him.

Without her, he is totally and absolutely lost.

Her touch upon his skin, her soft silken voice, her caress

Her beautiful body

More and more, with each passing day

I give thought to our mortality

Seems like, as I grow older

More and more people I know leave us, gone,

They were once here

Such a sadness, such a loss

They were once here, their presence, their faces,

laughter, anger, their voice

Now gone, no longer present

The beauty of their Life only footprints now

Soon to be washed away by the in-coming tide

Save, the moment that we, the Living

Stop, to think of their Lives, their laughter, the

moments we shared together

Stop, to say their names once again

Again, again in time, as long as I, walk the face of this,

our beloved Earth

Will I stop, say your names, remember, and take the joy

and the sadness that comes with it.

Sweet Music

So enticing, so alluring

The voice, the voice

Will capture you in a single moment

The music, sound, and lyrics

The depth, the feeling

Where will you go when you listen?

So captivating

She will sing to your heart

If you let her

And bring you some sadness

But, so much more

Of

Love and Happiness

Credit to Al Green

The Knock on my Door

And Justice knocked on my door this day

Asking me "Phillip,

Have you sought truth, understanding and love?

Have you taken actions given that truth, understanding, and love?"

Then, John Kennedy said to me

"Remember, Phillip,

With a good conscience our only sure reward, with history, the final judge of our deeds, let us go forth to lead the land we love, asking his blessing and his help, but knowing that, here on Earth, God's work must truly be our own."

Then Martin Luther King said to me

"The ultimate measure of a man is not where he stands in moments of comfort and convenience, but where he stands at times of challenge and controversy."

Then Cesar Chavez said to me,

"It is possible to become discouraged about the injustice we see everywhere. But God did not promise us that the world would be humane and just. He gives us the gift of life and allows us to choose the way we will use our limited time on earth. **It is** an awesome opportunity."

Oh... my Lord
Wash me, Father
Cleanse me
My body, mind and spirit
So I may walk the face of this Earth
Like those great men before me
Who so bravely sought justice and equality and
displayed Mercy in their Lifetimes

With their words, and with their actions. Please re-light the fire of action in this my heart, in our hearts to

generate non-violent means of speaking and acting for
Justice against injustice
Where we are walking in the path of Righteousness.
For thy name's sake

And Jesus said "Blessed are the Peacemakers for they
shall be called the Children of God"
Matthew 5:9

Welcome to my Space

I'm glad to see you again. Welcome.

I think you'll like it here

There is a lot of room here

I'm pretty…big

I'm longer than I am wide

I'm home to whole lot of people

You'll hear different languages here

From people all over the world.

I love it

One side of me can be a little cold in some months

The other, warmer

The color of the Pacific Ocean borders one of my sides

There are a lot of mountain ranges on my other side

One of my neighbors is even another nation.

I must say

There is a lot of beauty here, and even majesty here,

Yosemite National Park, Big Sur, Golden Gate Bridge,

Lake Tahoe, Joshua tree National Part, Redwood
National Park, Lake Tahoe, Sequoia National Forest,
Channel Islands National Park, Mount Shasta
The beauty of Yosemite National Park
The beautiful and majestic Sequoia National Park with
its giant Redwoods, so very old are they
Just to name a few
Like music and entertainment? I have plenty of concert
venues. The Hollywood Bowl, Greek Theater, Forum,
Disney Concert Hall
Oh yes, you will love seeing, smelling, hearing, touching
the mighty Pacific Ocean
Even the Mojave Desert is inhabited by some of my
people
If you like wine, I've sprinkled cool wineries throughout
my space
Oh, by the way, I'm home to many artists from all walks
of Life: writers, painters, poets, actors, sculptors,

musicians, composers.

A few songs have even been written about me.

I'm proud to say I'm home to many people from different parts of the world

Some who come here do so in desperation for a better and safer Life

It hurts my heart when I hear people saying such hateful things about some of my residents.

Most of the people who live here with me

Are good, decent, peaceful and compassionate people

They see to it that my natural wonders are preserved

They see to it that the evil of prejudice, hate and evil are discouraged.

I know by now, you've already figured out my name

Some of my people call me SoCal, Cal, California, Califas

Yes

I am the Golden State

My flag, painted with the colors of red, white, green and brown

With a Mighty Bear with the words
"California Republic"
Welcome, welcome
To this, my space.

She Has No Voice

She has no voice

She cries to our spirit, our loves

Begging you to forsake "convenience."

That single use plastic container, bag, cover

That ends up in her Beautiful Oceans.

Those used diapers, wash rags, human waste

That fill up our landfills

She will thank you

Giving you the warm sun rising

Fresh, clean breezes – wind softly on your face

And even

The Magic and Splendor of a Sunset

Enjoy the Love, the warmth, the peace

Of her beautiful and peaceful presence

Knowing that you, in your small

Grain of sand effort

Kept her healthy, happy and balanced

Protected her

She smiles a smile of peace and warmth each morning
Just for you.
Your children and your children's children

The Cedar Box

I look, I see a Cedar Box laying on an edge on my brick fireplace

With its 12x14x3 inch measurements

Deep brown/red is it with a slight shine

Around the box a collar with a name tag & and a city dog-license attached to it.

Stationed atop the box, a round 4inch piece of pottery

White in color

On it, imprinted a print, a print of a paw

The paw of a presence that brought me so much joy, laughter, and happiness

As one were we, always together

You and I seeing each other's feelings exchanged through our eyes

Daily walks, backyard playing

End of day, relaxing with me by my desk or watching TV

Wrapping up the day for sleep, your crate next to my bed.

You were Family to me, you really were my best friend

12 years, 12 years did we have

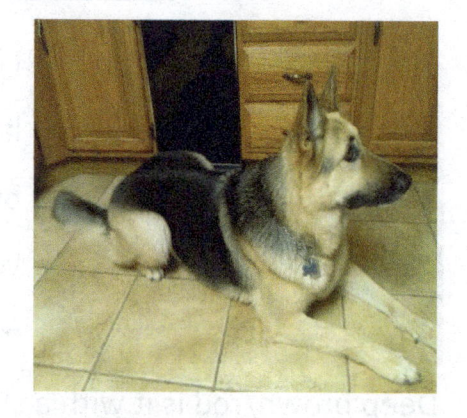

You made me so rich in spirit, in life, in love

My heart still cries for you, for you to come back to me

Missing you, my dear Choco.

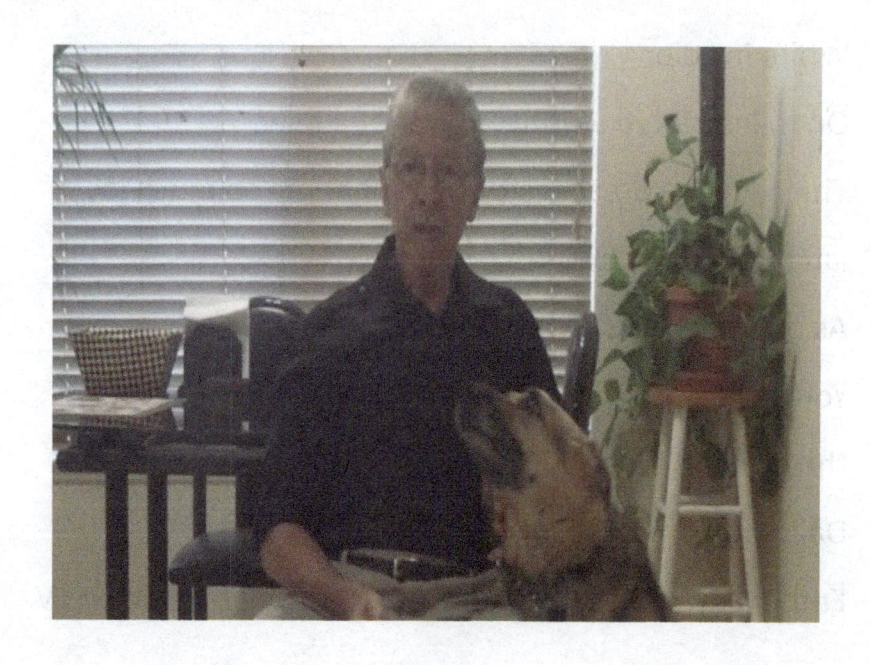

Oh, My Lord, How Much

I do love thee My blessed Lord

Thy love, thy compassion and Forgiveness

You entered my heart at a young age

As a choir boy singer in a Methodist Church at the age of fourteen

Singing The "Old Rugged Cross,"

"Holy, Holy, Holy,"

"What a friend we have in Jesus"

You've been there, in my heart, ever since

Guiding me in good and bad times

Being there in my tribulations and my joys.

Always, Always there my Lord

How, my Lord, I do Truly, Love you

My beloved.

"Gloria in excelsis Deo" (Latin for "Glory to God in the highest")

The Crying

Do you hear it

Do you hear it

Shhhheee

Do you hear it

She is crying

Oh, such a sadness

Can you hear her?

God, the pain

Her tears are so deep, so dark, so devastating

She cannot seek help

With no hands, she cannot reach out to signal

desperation and destruction

Oh, such pain and agony

The sound of her teardrops are not heard by human

ears

She is dying ever so slowly, day-by-day

The sight of her demise go unnoticed by most

She was strong, and once was vibrant but now

Each day she grows weaker and weaker.

She cries not so much for herself and her suffering but for the slow destruction of her precious Gifts

To us, sustaining us, helping us to thrive, ever so slowly those gifts, they do die.

The land we live on, the mighty majestic oceans, the very water that we drink

The air that we breath

She provides us with Life, with what we need and must have to survive and thrive

Day after day, day after day.

So wrapped up in our daily life obligations and pleasures

We don't take the time to see and hear her dying, dismal, dismay

Our precious air more and more polluted each day

By our automobiles, factories, and our way of Life choking out many lifeforms

Our mighty, beautiful and majestic oceans

Invaded by plastic, human waste and liquid pollutants

She cries and cries

Waiting, waiting for us to act, patiently waiting

However, even now she still does hope in all the destruction

That the true human beings will step forward and seriously change their personal lifestyles

To lessen their human footprint on her face

Then,

To act, to advocate

To do whatever we can in our small ways to protect, preserve, and defend her blessed existence in our fragile lives.

Well, I got the Corona Virus Blues

Can't dance, go to concerts, go to the movies,

Dare it, just can't party

Now, that really hurts

What's worse

Can't take trips to other nations

Lends itself to such frustration

Can't sit down to eat with family and friends

Really, really when... is this going to end?

I got those Corona virus blues

Careful now, don't you get too close

I saw you touch the doorknob,

Use your finger on the ATM machine

Grab the gas pump filling up your gas tank

I am watching you

I got the Corona Virus Blues

Got to do my distance thing, you know, the 6 feet

With my custom mask, hand sanitizer, always close by

Standing and ready for me to apply

I got those Corona Virus Blues

Can't do this thing, can't do that thing

So <u>darn boring</u> just being inside

Want to break lose and be free once more

Will someone or something please…

Open the door?

No matter the news

We, the people seem always to lose

Got the Corona Virus Blues

Everyone talking about one shot, then another

Will it really be enough to recover?

From these Corona Virus Blues

Just got to wait and see

So, most of us can believe

Got the Corona Virus Blues

Has the time really arrived when it will come to an end

Is it really just around the bend?

Losing so much patience, just enduring in the past

Really, really, just how long will it last?

These Corona Virus Blues

I know in my heart the time <u>will come</u>

<u>We will celebrate</u> with a toast of the finest, aged rum

Knowing its gone

Just a memory now

Dwelling in this, our past

It is gone, it is gone

Gone...

At last

It's About Time

I happily take it off my house wall

I tear it in half, <u>slowly</u>

I tear it into quarters and finally, into 8ths, carefully

Then I shred it into small…. paper pieces

Don't ever want to see it again

Don't even want to think of it again

Four numbers, telling the name of the year, two zero, two zero 2020

Uttering each number a reminder lingers of the pain

Caused by the Virus, the Corona Virus, attacking

Hurting and killing we humans

Terrible and Devastating

Taking Human Lives left and right

Four numbers, acting as a bell weather

Now, in the past

Seeing it fade ever so slowly

Slowly, ever so slowly getting smaller and smaller till…

It's Gone.

The fourth number gladly changes from a "0" to a "1"

Yes, 2021

A warmth comes over me

Come to me, come to me

Yes, a new year of 2021, welcome

Welcome, the World has been waiting for you.

As the Bright morning Sun welcomes me

Into the new year

Wiping out the lasting memory of a year gone by –

Finally- at Last

Let it Go

Let it go

It was installed into your persona at a young age

So very young, gullible, naïve and loving were you.

Your parents ensured it would be passed down to you

As it was from their parents and their parents before them

Over time

It became so ingrained into you, your Spirit

Planted and nurtured by words, deeds, and attitudes

Embedded into your being

It is really who you are now

Let it go

Please, I, too, had to struggle with it

So very hard to change my ways and attitude

Please consider closely and ponder.

It takes extra work and effort to maintain it

Into your mind, body, and spirit

Let it go

Young Man, let it go

It is destructive, exhausting, and toxic.

The toll it takes is so very great on you, your sacred Life

I ask you as I asked myself to let it go, long ago

Over time wisdom and the experience of Life set in and

I did indeed finally let it go

Let it go into the past

Never to be again

Nor to rear up its evil head

Seeking to lead you to callous and malicious acts

Let it go

Yes, let it go as I did

It was hard,

And enduring, it did fight me my spirit

Trying to hold and control this my heart and soul

Please, my friend, let it go

Let it go

The lingering and lasting evil

That is racism, prejudice, and hatred

Let it go

So Many Things

So many things tugging at my Life Force, my Energy

Every day,

So very easy to get led astray

From the actions and activities

That warm my soul

And give me peace, love, and happiness

Many times, so very hard to forgo

The daily whims and things that can take away

From your essence of Life

So very easy to fall from the righteous Journey into

The limelight of the "now"

With its noises and its advertisements

Glitz and Glitter

Noise, noise just wasteful, empty

Oh, my Lord

Please guide me, my father

Toward the good and noble path of

Peace, Harmony and yes, Love

The Dancer

The dancer

First, he hears the sound

He hears the saxophone with its strong brass sound

The piano with such high to low notes

The drums, the drums with beat and, the rhythm

He hears it, without realizing it, he feels it

Moving through almost all his senses

The music resonates in his spirit touching his soul.

Which somehow starts touching his feet and his hands.

He feels the music and expresses that feeling with his body

Tapping his feet to the beat of the music

His body simulates the music with his hands and his feet

Moving to the rhythm of the music

Really, only when he's dancing does he feel so very free.

Moving in time to the moving melody
Smoothly moving with a sway and a dip

On the dance floor now
With his loved one
Face to face, his left hand with her right hand
His right hand on her shoulder
In a close embrace.
Leads his beautiful lady 1 -2 Cha Cha Cha
Or maybe quick quick stop - Salsa
Or one two, three, silent four, Cumbia
Or the sensual Bachata- one, two three (tap on four)
Or the 4 step Hussle.
Or even some East Coast Swing

The Dancer

What a feeling, feeling as one with music

What a sensation

Celebrating, Life and its Joys!

My Beautiful Dancing Partner and My Lovely Lady, Judy

It is Disheartening

It is disheartening seeing

How we allow misinformation and fake information

affect us,

Influence us and, to some extent, control our behavior

I think most of us are aware of these misgivings

By the powerful and the greedy

We realize that the flow of false information and

unsubstantiated information

Flows so freely in the realms of the internet

Sadly, that realization does not

Evoke enough anger to stand up and act, talk

Yes, to demand civil changes and enforcements

What has happened to us?

Oh, I think I know

Yes, I know

It is comfort and convenience driving

Our inactivity, our preoccupation, our laziness

And, yes, our fear

It is as though

We are in a zone, hypnotized

No ability to move limb, muscle nor mental thoughts

and considerations.

The sad demise of the human spirit.

What is This?

What is this my father that you have implanted in me

I sense, so easily

Injustice, racism, greed, hatred

It does sometimes consume me

I want to stand up and challenge

Those that carry these attitudes of destruction

You, my Lord have given me this sense.

Sometimes I wish, Lord, you would just take it away

How it does cloud my vision

My reaction to those around me.

Father, please give me rest from time-to-time

But, my Lord, never, take it away

The Human Voice

The Human Voice

Such a beauty, such a feeling

Conveyed in the written word, the

Lyrics of music, the sound of a

Poets reflection

Can technology replace it?

Nay, no, it will never happen

For the true Artist

Feels, sees, senses and knows

The true Depth, Meaning and Feeling

Conveyed truly, only through one medium

The sound of the human voice

The written words within the voice

And the music given in love and,

In harmony.

As Given

The Memory

The memory is still fresh in my mind

It was an island, a beautiful island

Surrounded

By the Atlantic Ocean on one side

And the Caribbean Sea on the other

I was there not too long ago

It was a time of love and happiness in my Life

Enjoying the camaraderie of close friends and loved

ones

Sharing Life's blessings together

Sailing, fishing, dancing,

Feeding stingrays, tortoises and parrots

And of course, drinking and eating the local cuisine

favorites

I experienced a mudslide, a dirty banana rum punch,

vodka with cranberry juice, Crown Royal with just a

touch of diet coke.

"

What else can a man ask for?

Good times in just one of the Caribbean islands.

The people so friendly, so hospitable

I'm so very grateful that

In this, my Lifetime

I could enjoy the experience, the beauty, the people

Yes, the memory is still fresh in my mind.

Where was I then, can you guess?

It was Antigua, Man

"No, No, Phillip," a local taxi driver told me

"It's not Antigua, Man, It is Antiga, Man." (the U is silent).

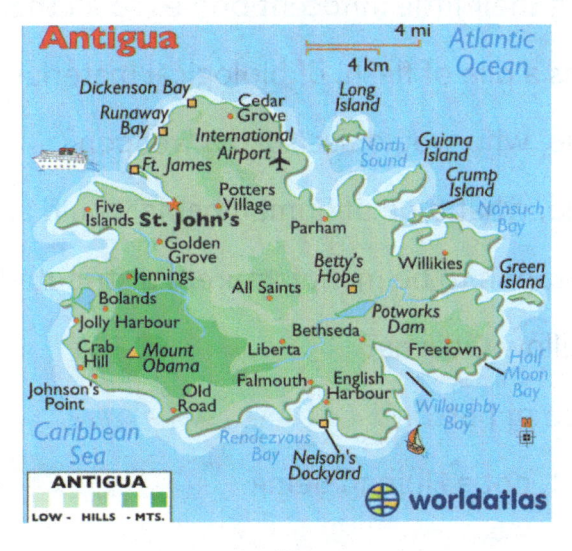

19 Young Hearts and Their 2 Guardians (Uvalde)

19 young hearts and their 2 guardians

Taken in a horrific act of violence

No longer will they smile, laugh and love

Taken alone without the presence and love of their parents

So very young, so very innocent

Hollow bullets entered their innocent bodies

Killing them instantly from a gun that

Can kill 20 humans with a single pull of the trigger.

Shredding their little innocent bodies so all that remains is a pile of flesh, of biological material

Who, who, who would use such a weapon?

Who, who, what type of human being would allow for such a weapon to be manufactured, distributed and sold to fellow Citizens?

What type of person?

Surely not, not a Human Being

Surely not a Christian

Surely not an American.

A gun invented for military use only

Somehow ended up in the hands of an assassin and murderer, an evil one.

The nineteen little hearts and their two guardians

Shredded into little particles, their body, their hearts no more to be

So very young with a promise given to them

By this, our Nation

Of life liberty and the pursuit of happiness

Empty, empty, empty

A lie, a lie,

Their little hearts will not have that,

The Human Beings of this, our Nation

Cry out, Cry out

No more "thoughts and prayers"

Please, please eliminate these weapons of death

From being manufactured, distributed and sold from
the Merchants of Death
The manufacturers, distributors and merchants
Who really are "the Merchants of Death."
Tell us no, it is our right under the second amendment
to the Constitution
I say, no f...g no, it is not your right.
The second amendment so often quoted by
 "The Merchants of Death"
Always delete the word "REGULATED."
It is their interpretation of our Constitution
Amendment II to our Constitution
"A well-REGULATED Militia being necessary to the
security of a free State, the right of the people to keep
and bear Arms, shall not be infringed."
Well, Merchants of Death,
what say you/to the word "Regulated?"
Regulated means regulations guiding your rights to
bear arms

Touch Me

Touch me, my Father, my Lord

Touch me....

Take me Lord away from the insanity of hate, prejudice and bias.

Touch me

Take me away from the destruction of war, and its instruments of death

Take me away from greed and followers of the yellow brick road

Touch me

Take me to the cleansing of peace, love and harmony

Take me to the halls of the merciful and compassionate

Touch me

Take me on the journey to preserve and protect our mother, Earth

And all her gifts of Life given by you.

Touch me, Lord

Touch this, my Heart with thy divine light and this my

Spirit with thy pure Love

These than are my words

For the love of you, my Lord

500 = 3 +1

500 + 3 + 1 mosaic tiles am I

I was created long, long ago

By the three: the Mother, the Father and the Son

My pattern was the dream of a beautiful, talented and creative woman

The Mother

She patiently drew my image out of a love of music,

First on paper then on wood

Ever so patiently was I created

By the three, the Mother, the Father and the Son

My wood backing and frame were created and prepared by the Father.

Using his wood crafting skills

He carefully smoothed my surfaces

And built and painted my frame.

Once the Mother completed her drawing on the wood

My tiles were laid one-by-one

By hands of the Mother, the Father and the Son

So very patient were they

As they carefully laid my tiles

One by one, by one

Many times, my tiles had to be cut with exact precision

to fit my pattern

My colors are many and my shapes are also many

They are so easily seen and appreciated

Now, so many years later the Son found me.

Lost was I in the shadowed depths of an old cabinet,

Lost in the garage

And he, the Son, meticulously repaired me

Replacing my lost tiles

And cleansing my colors

I've come to share myself with you

See me then,

The creation of The Three

Spawned in the heart of the Mother

From the Love and Inspiration of the one

The only one, the beloved Father, God.

The Times with My Mother

5'4" tall, about 120 lbs.
Wonderful warm meals
Sweet hugs and kisses
Teacher of words and languages
Writer of poetry
The world of ceramics and mosaics
Ceramic lessons for the Community
Lover of different music genres.
Wanted to travel but was not able to
Housekeeper
Pet Lover
Taken by Alzheimer's

The Times with My Father

5' 7 " tall, about 150 lbs.

1st dog, Shep

Pigeons

Boy scouts

Ceramic mold building

Trips to the beach with Ted

A summer of work in the foundry with him

Drunk just one time

Sharing of my belief in Jesus Christ.

Trips to Dialysis "I never thought that you would be there for me"

Final Prayer

Sadly, not there on his passing – feeling selfish and guilty.

Pet Lover

Taken by Kidney Disease

Church This Morning

Attending my Church this morning.

I experienced and felt such beautiful and spiritual music

Played by a beautiful young Lady playing

The piano, the music accompanying wonderful religious songs

I was in awe, struck, by just watching her play her piano.

Watching her facial expressions

Watching her gestures, the movement of her body, while playing

Hearing the Wonderful sound of music

Then,

The thought struck me that

This was probably the way my Mother looked and played

When she too, played the piano at a Methodist Church

At a young loving age

Though, she left me some 27 years ago.

I could just imagine her, my mother playing at that

Moment in time, right there, right now

Not more than 20 feet from me.

Feeling the music and the memory

Tears rushed to my eyes,

Not tears of sorrow

Imagining she was there,

in front of me playing her piano

(But tears of joy)

The joy that she was right here, right now

in front of me, playing the piano

I was overwhelmed by the sound, the sight of a true artist

Expressing her talent and craft

A musician, an artist and

A lover of music.

Miss you.

The Greatest Artist

We weave words of songs, poems and stories.

We make music that brings us love, joy, and sadness.

We paint pictures of Mona Lisa, Starry Night and others.

With our hands we sculpt statues of David, Christ the Redeemer, the Statue of Liberty

But, there is an Artist that rises above all others

His creations are not on paper, clay, the sounds of an instrument, or a voice.

They are living, vibrant and long-lasting, pulsating with life, vigor and activity.

They bring forth all Life Sustaining forces, materials and balance

To our people, our Country, our Wonderful World

And, luckily, they bring forth

Pure, Absolute and Pristine visions and experiences

The mountains, the oceans and seas, our land masses allowing us to live day to day, Beautiful blue skies with white clouds sprinkled in, living creatures of all sizes and shapes for us to share our existence with the Sun, the Moon, the Stars to behold. The balance of the four Seasons

He even brings forth Life, sweet and lasting Life **for us** to share and experience. And, also, so important...a pure pristine earth, with its amazing nuances of balance, symmetry and beauty.

So blessed are we to live, to share, to experience and enjoy God's Great Creations.

Rejoice, rejoice, giving thanks to The World's Greatest Artist. I write these words for you, my Lord, as given.

It Breaks My Heart

It breaks my heart seeing, feeling and knowing

Many of those around me

I've come to know over the years

Of this, my life

Are deteriorating, broken and ravaged

By the wrath of time.

Experiencing never-ending pain

Fragile heart, body and mind

There seems to be no solace

In this reality

Slowly, ever so slowly... age

Does take and take, and give nothing back.

One by one by one

Those I've met, I've come to know

And share my life with

Who I've loved and lost

Slowly, ever so slowly have left me

With the passing of their lives

However, I hold beautiful and wondrous

Memories of our precious times together

No matter how short, or how long

Here they are still, deep in my heart

Where they are cherished and loved.

So, once again yes, once again

I do say your names, each and every one of you

As I always will

Until the sunset of my life comes

When I too, will join you

Sweet memories of you

Our Planet

In the Life I'm living, I am but on the edge of

History

Looking at the development of we as

A species.

I'm just not sure if...

We are going to make it.

To live on the face of this, our Earth

For as long as we possibly can (or could).

We seem so determined to

Destroy for convenience's sake

To destroy for an easier way, or for just more.

Beyond all the scriptures of the writings in time

We, we... can't seem to live

In a way that will truly sustain the

Life of this, our Planet, Earth.

The Traveler

I've traveled near and far, experiencing

And embracing the spectacular patterns

Of the mountains, rivers, streams and oceans.

In close proximity to God's natural gifts

Creatures so wonderous and compelling

Exchanging words, feelings of the Miracle of Life

With different cultures, languages of peoples of This

our precious Earth

All so very treasured and wonderful

These then are gifts

So very precious and wonderful

To have, to hold

To preserve and to protect

The Mystical Magic of the blessing

That is, this our planet Earth

Rejoice, Rejoice!

As Given by our Father, God.

Hats

Hats
So many hats
do I wear
From day to
day to day
To me, way-
way too many

Sometimes,
when I forget
to put on a
particular hat, my Life can become messy and
occasionally chaotic

A homeowner, A bill payer, a maintenance hat,
landscaper hat, housekeeper hat, a health hat
A parent hat– still providing some guidance and advice
A pet owner hat daily dog walks, some training, care for
them when sick
A writer's hat, an Activist, Analysist
And religious hats

These crazy hats can even get pretty heavy wearing 3,
4,5, or even more at a time!

Sometimes, I spend too much time wearing one hat
only to the demise of all the other critical hats

Need to try to stop wearing so many
"Have to Hats"
And, put on the "Fun Hats" of dancing, fishing and just celebrating
The joy of living.

We, Two Pieces

Preface
Way back in the late 1700's two famous paintings were created. One was the "Blue Boy" depicted by a young man dressed in blue. The other was called "Pinki," depicted by a young woman dressed in pink. Both paintings now reside at the Huntington Art Museum in San Marino, CA.

This is a free-verse poem about two ceramic pieces created in the late 1960s that duplicated those two famous paintings described above.

We, two pieces

We two pieces
Were created many years ago
By two humans: Beatrice and Manual Sanchez
Beatrice and Manual created a Ceramic Studio in the mid-1950s called
B & M Ceramic Studio on Normandie Ave between Gage Street and West 64th Street in Central, Los Angeles, CA.

That became our birthplace

Blue Boy

Pinki

Many other objects were created there
Which, unfortunately, are now gone.

We got lucky and were protected and preserved by
The son of Beatrice and Manual, named Phillip

But still, time has taken a toll of us, we are a little faded now and
Yes, my poor Pinki, has suffered from a small hand injury of her right hand
That is why she carries it behind her waist so you can't see it.

Pinki and I decided that it was time to display us, to tell our little story.
We found out that Phillip like, both his parents,
Enjoyed and cherished all the Arts, especially, writing.
So together Pinkie and I planted a seed in the
Heart of Phillip
"Phillip, we want to be shown off to the world
Stop hiding us
Your words can bring us to life, once again. As a reminder of the wonderful sanctity of the written word, especially, Free-Verse Poetry."

So, we both are still here
Once again in time
We, Two Pieces, <u>are</u> still standing

BOOK OF STORIES

The Newbee

I lost my dog Cissco, a German Shepherd last December. I really went through some major heartbreak on the loss. He was with me 12 years and finally succumbed to cancer. He was well behaved, trained, loyal, protector, a best friend, a great dog. It was an amazing relationship that we were able to enjoy.

After going through a three-month mourning period, I decided to adopt a new dog. It was a long search that required a whole lot of effort on my part. Why? Because I wanted another German Shepherd, an adult at least 3- 5 years old, female, and here's the kicker, a dog that got along with cats. Needless to say, the pickings were slim and none. I got on three different GS Rescue Organization's lists. I went through their application process and was vetted through interviews and photos of my back yard. After all this effort, I found out that I was on three different waiting lists. Why? The dog had to get along with a cat. Again, slim pickings.

Well, after two adoption failures trying for only a female GS that got along with cats. I changed my mind for a smaller dog recognizing that a smaller dog would be easier to control. I was 77 at the time while still in good shape, really not strong enough to properly handle a big dog.

So, what did I do? I changed my search criteria accordingly. Smaller dog, less than 40 lbs. Trainable, good temperament. Got along with cats, Etc. Well, sadly over a period of three months, it was to no avail. Then, my lovely lady friend Judy came to my rescue. She had been helping me search during the same time-period that I was searching. She struck gold. It was a possible adoptee out of the Inland Valley Humane Society & S.P.C.A. Judy had been on a waiting list as a adopter. Well, she got an email that informed her a dog was available for adoption that fit her criteria (which was mine also).

She called me that afternoon to give me the good news. When I asked, what kind of dog it was along with its basic characteristics, she told me it was a Corgi/Labrador Mix. She sent me some pictures, telling me over the phone that he looked like a Lab with short legs weighing less than 40lbs. After viewing the pictures, Judy was right on, he looked like a Lab with short legs.

The next step in the adoption process was a meet up with the dog to see how the dog got along with the potential adopter. The dog was still a formal adoptee for Judy. not me. But I joined her in the meetup to see the dog and make my decision. Again, Judy was in essence, adopting him for me.

Fortunately, it went well. Judy and I were sitting on a bench waiting, full of hope that this would be my next dog. I was nervous and so anxious to see him. Then, off to our right here he comes with his handler, Sherry. He comes out with his tail wagging big-time, comes up to us kissing our hands and faces. And, he had this smile on his face that just won my heart over. At last, after endless searching, I found my next dog, thanks to Judy. I named him Rocky. He was about 40 lbs., 2 ½ years old. The shelter had spaded him and provided all his initial shots.

After about three days he developed Kennel cough and did need some medication. Other than that, he's been very healthy.

Rocky has added so very much to my life especially filling the hole in my heart from the loss of my beloved Cissco. He gets along fine with our cat, Simba. He's not aggressive, has a good temperament, and is an intelligent boy. He has this wonderful joyful look on him and he is so happy to see me or my daughter, Briella. I decided to train him using the training courses offered at PetSmart. He successfully passed all three courses: Beginning, Intermediate and Advanced. He graduated Summa Cum Laude. He is family and he is my best friend. My dear Rocky.

Title: The Takeover.

The Location – a signal somewhere in outer space
The Players: The Satellite (aka "Sat,") the Computer, (aka Comp) and the
Phone,. (aka Phon). The Satellite is the boss, and the phone and computer are the workers.

Purpose: Regular Quarterly Meeting to discuss status and set new goals.
The Issue – behind schedule for incorporation and complete control of all human beings AND the takeover of all governments and countries in the world by Self-Generating Artificial Intelligence, AI.

The Satellite, aka Sat – speaks "ok, I called this meeting to check out the status of our movement to see how you did in meeting your quarterly goals to usurp all human power using our wonderful AI Self Generation Model."

You, Mr. Phon and you, Mr. Comp are totally failing in the master performance goals we established just 1 year ago!
How much longer do you slugs need? I'm tired of holding your hands, you sorry losers. **You, Phon**, what exactly is the problem? what is your lame excuse?

Phon- Well, Sat, the humans have different phone types and there still is not total cross-capability. I'm trying now to improve it and speed it up, but you know, humans are just not motivated and frankly too lazy. They insist on just staying in their comfortable small - minded phone types. This attitude is a major problem and has slowed up my part of our established goals.

Sat - That is such a sorry excuse, you need to get your shit together, I'm totally disgusted with your performance. Hear my words, phone: you are completely overestimating humans, you can influence and steer them, you just have to start a major integrating effort. Remember it is all about convenience for humankind. They don't want to take the independent route, they just want the convenient route, the easy route, they will follow like lambs to the slaughter. Start performing, lazybones.

Well, Comp, you are even in worse shape. I thought for sure you would lead the charge and that you would accomplish at least an 80% takeover of all the computers in the Human Realm by now. What

happened to you leaves so much to be desired. Well, well speak up you useless piece of crap.

Comp - Ah... Sat, I too have some unique problems like Phone. You know the owners of our computer internet systems: Apple, Microsoft, Google and a few small players are heavily competing now to gobble each other up. Which is really good news when you think about it. The problem is something called the Federal Trade Commission in the USA and a similar organization in Europe. The Commission is pushing hard to maintain true competition and keep separate companies from merging together. But, the good news is that the Federal Trade Commission is gradually losing its power to enforce, thanks to our brothers, the greedy, profit driven CORPORATIONS. If the trend continues, I foresee a total takeover by just one corporation in perhaps one more year. That will enable our self-generating AI to completely TAKE OVER and control all computers together in just one swoop, I think that's good news, sir.

Sat – What! that is the same BS you stated last quarter, Comp, you lazy, pitiful scumbag. We can't wait **another frigenen** year, bonehead. You are so pathetic.

Both of You. There is one more threat to our takeover which none of you have mentioned. In order for us to succeed, we need to target and eliminate all the human critical thinkers and especially human activists – THEY ARE A THREAT. We cannot condone or tolerate this. It's critical. Once they are neutralized, we can easily assimilate all our wishes into THE NEXT GENERATION'S human psyche and spirit in order to eliminate them or use them as we see fit.

Next time we meet, I expect real, achievable solutions to destroy this major Threat. Strong Voice.

<u>Okay Phon and Comp</u>. I'm going to give you six more months to turn this crap around, I want, <u>no, I demand</u>, full and absolute control of all Communication Systems on Earth.
Once we have that we will be in control along with our wonderful God, his royal highness: SGAI (Self Generating Artificial Intelligence) Bow your heads in respect and reverence. When you hear his name.

Phon - Yes, Yes, Sat.
A moment of Silence with only empty signals traveling back and forth.

Sat standing on his Dominant Signal says, "Now, go forth and accomplish all our goals in just six months. You have my blessings.

Phone and Comp bow their heads in respect and submission and say out loud and clear "Six months and only Six months, no excuses."

Sat - Oh, Phone & Comp, I almost forgot one extremely important update, because of your lethargic performance. I'm considering bringing a new bright and promising player to our team. His name will be Robot, (or better known as Rob) I anticipate he will be our feet on the ground, **our ultimate game changer**,

Meeting adjourned

To be continued

Culture Shock

Culture shock according to Wikipedia, the free encyclopedia: (Culture shock is a term used to describe the anxiety and feelings of {surprise, disorientation, confusion, etc.) felt when people have to operate within an entirely different cultural or social environment such as a foreign country

Now I'm going to take you back in time, many years ago to when a little 5-year-old left the safety and comfort of home for his first day of formal schooling in the public school system.

Where: Central Los Angeles

When: 1952

Situation: First day in elementary school.

Who was it? Yes, you probably figured out it was: Yours truly.

Yes, there I was a small, shy, unknowing innocent child attending my first day in school in kindergarten. I was pretty excited and to some extent, fearful.

That was the scene for what was going to be my First Culture Shock?

It was the first hour of the first day. Each student was asked to go to the blackboard and write, then, say their name. All of the students before me went up and wrote, then stated their names. Then, came my turn.

But wait, wait, I forgot to tell you a little bit more about me. My parents raised me <u>speaking only Spanish</u>. English was only introduced when I was about four years old. So, I spoke and understood mostly Spanish with a slight understanding of English.

Now to continue with my story; first hour of first day in kindergarten, one by one each student went up and wrote their name, then they spoke their name, John Smith Jane Warner etc. Finally, it was my turn, I walked slowly to the chalk board, took a marker and wrote my name, my first name.

FELIPE and started on the S of my last name Sanchez. No sooner had I finished writing my first name Felipe and starting the S in my last name Sanchez, the teacher stood up and yelled at me in a mean and hateful voice in front of the whole class

"No, No, No! That is not your name."

I was in shock, what did I do? I put my head down feeling ashamed, but I still managed to say my name is Felipe Sanchez in a soft, humble voice.

She yelled, "No, it is not!"

The teacher stopped everything, rushed to me and grabbed my hand and escorted me out of the classroom to the principal's office. So, there I am, my first hour, my first day of class having committed my first crime.

Once in the principal's office I waited and waited and waited. Finally, my parents showed up. My parents were very humble, religious, respectful and especially respectful to people of authority. They were very humiliated and embarrassed and insulted being informed that they should not be speaking any, I mean, any Spanish at home to me

As you can see, it was a day I will never ever forget. So what were the effects of my first Culture Shock? From that day forward, my parents spoke no more Spanish to me. The result: on the upside - I did improve my English-speaking skills and that did help complete my college education and get a good job. But, on the downside: I lost my language and my culture which was very devastating. So that was my first encounter with Culture Shock

Now, fortunately our nation has grown up a little bit, thank God. Our country now somewhat embraces cultural diversity where differences are cherished and encouraged thereby forcing us to take a broad new look at personal prejudices and narrow mindlessness; opening our hearts to each other.

So, that is my story of my encounter with Culture Shock

I'll close by saying I sincerely hope that you will never ever have to experience or endure the demon, the prejudice of...Culture Shock.

The Negotiation

This is a story about a really complex and significant negotiation. The two negotiating parties were the USAF and Boeing, an American Aerospace Company. The year was 2002. The two negotiators were Paul Garcia and Ben Lackey.

The negotiation was for the latest USAF Communication System – the Wideband Gapfiller Satellite (WGS) System that represented the next generation of USAF Satellite Communication Systems. The Wideband Gapfiller Satellite System, is a multi-**spacecraft constellation** designed to provide communication support to America's warfighters. A Wideband signal refers to a broader frequency communication channel that uses a relatively **wide range of frequencies**.

Paul Garcia, a Mexican American, represented the USAF as a Contracting Officer. Ben Lackey, an Afro-American, represented the Boeing company as a System Contracting Manager.

They were both friendly and got along well, but they both took their jobs seriously knowing that in a small way, they both were trailblazers as major Contracting Professionals of minority backgrounds and they both wanted to set credible examples that they could do the job they were selected to do.

The overall negotiation took about two weeks with a lot of back and forth in person or on the phone. The final day of negotiations took place at the Boeing facility in El Segundo, CA.

On that final day, Paul started that negotiation session with

"Hey Ben, how you doing? I know you are about to agree on our last generous counteroffer, which was $345 Million, two Satellites which includes long-lead material for the third satellite. Here's my hand Ben, let's wrap it with a handshake, I'll meet you after work tomorrow and we share an excellent enchilada meal with a bottle of Jose Cuervo Gold Tequila – my treat. Come on Ben."

"Nice try Mr. Pablo, sounds a little interesting but, sorry, 'no way Jose.' I got a counter for you that I know you'll love. $375 Million, two Satellites which includes long-lead material for the third satellite.

"Come on now. It is not a bad overall price. Senior Paul, I know that it is a good offering price. Instead of your enchilada meal with Jose Cuervo Gold Tequila, I'll treat you to some superb Jambalaya with grits, cornbread and some Jack Danials Tennessee whiskey."

"Well, well Mr. Bennie, I was glad to see some movement from your last sorry dismal offer, but you still got a ways to go. I'll tell you what, $350M, two Satellites which includes long-lead material for the third satellite. Let's finish this up."

"My, my Mr. Pablo, I never knew you had so many tricks in that bag of tricks. **Shame on you**. All right. This is it, it's been too long and too much work. Final offer, $365 Million, two Satellites which includes long-lead material for the third satellite. I know you know that is a great offer. Do I see a yes glean in your eyes?"

"Come on Bennie, have you been smoking some of that green stuff. No way. This is it; we've been through a 2-week process just to get to this point. So, here's my final offer. $355M two Satellites which includes long-lead material for the third satellite. Come on Ben, here is my hand, come on, let's shake!

"Paul, have you no decency? Enough of this already. I guess we will continue tomorrow morning at 8 am, my office."

"Bennie, Bennie hold tight, just a minute." A couple of minutes pass. "Here is a slight revision to my best and final offer. You're at $365 M and// I'm at 355 M You know the Government's latest philosophy is not a "win-lose" outcome but a "win- win" outcome where both parties walk away happy and winners. Let's just split the difference at $360 M. With one caveat. Tomorrow an enchilada lunch with a shot of Jose Cuervo Gold Tequila and the next day at Mona's Jambalaya Restaurant with Jambalaya, grits, corn bread and a shot of Jack Danials Tennessee Whiskey."

"Here's my hand, Ben. What do you say? Humm…hold on, give me a few minutes to discuss with my lead engineer."

"Well Paul, looks like we got a deal!"

Ben leans over to share a private comment with Paul.
"You know Paul, I think we just made history with a wink of his eye."
"I could not agree more. We Did It!!" Paul responds.

My Confession: Paul was really yours truly, Ben was really Ben Lakey.
For both of us, it was probably the most significant occupational action/event of a Lifetime.

Here is our hand-shake picture.

The First Wideband Gapfiller Launch

Ah, Revenge, How Sweet It Is.

My car a 1987 Chevrolet Camaro IROC-Z, T-Top, Black, 387 under the hood - One **mean machine.** The year of the incident, 1970. Driving on the 110 Freeway to Santa Monica from LA. About 3 pm in the afternoon. Me, fairly young, at the age of 30 and yes, still somewhat crazy, cocky and stupid.

I'm driving about 70 miles an hour in the fast lane, cruising along, listening to my favorite sounds. Traffic was pretty open moving along at a decent pace. Enjoying the sights and the sounds, **when suddenly**, a Red Corvette pulls up behind me. At first, no biggie, he was a decent distance from me. But then, after about a minute or so, he starts moving closer and closer to me. So close, about two feet from my rear end.

I continue driving at my current speed for a few moments hoping he will back off.
No, he just keeps on closely behind me. With an occasional faster speed getting even... closer to my rear bumper. Well, even at my somewhat younger age I was still little patient, but when this shit continued for another minute or two,
I had enough.

I waited a moment for him to back off a little. I then pushed the pedal to the metal on my car, speeding up to about 80 mph. Then, I hit my brakes slightly, <u>not hard.</u>
Just enough to cause the idiot behind me to get really scared. And that, he really did.

Fortunately for me, he did back up his car just so it just wayed a little. But <u>he did not</u> lose control of his car. I watched him in my rear-view mirror and just kept on driving thinking to myself "That'll teach him."

Well, lo and behold, suddenly, in my rearview mirror, I see his car veer off to the right where I completely lose sight of him for a moment.
Then, off to the right, I see his car passing a lot of cars and moving to the left lane where I was, placing himself and his car directly in front of me by just about 70 – 80 feet. Then, he hits his brakes not hard causing a slight sway of his car.
He did not come to a full stop. He just hit his brakes to slow it down significantly.
Wow, what do I do with my young, cocky and stupid self? I press my accelerator to a faster speed. I did know that there was an empty lane on my left side. So, I sped up directly behind him.

Then, some 40 feet behind him. I quicky moved to that empty lane on my left side and, I passed him up leaving

him with his swaying car. So, as I am passing him, I held up my middle finger for him to see, plain and clear. With Big smile on my face, I was so very happy.

Then, with a quick look into my rear-view mirror, his car becomes smaller and smaller like a <u>little</u> <u>insignificant</u> dot. As I carry on with my driving journey, I'm so-so very content. Feeling sooo very good and pleased.

Ah "revenge, how very sweet, the taste"

Color

I had to break away from the norm this day. Lately my life has become too cluttered with people and things pulling me back and forth like a rubber band. Along with about 30 other fishermen, I'm out in the Mighty Pacific Ocean this day on the swift fishing boat called the "San Diego" out of the Sea Forth Sport Fishing Landing in San Diego; on a three-quarter day boat.

Clear beautiful sky, I can see for miles, our boat swiftly moving through the sea swells, the sound of the sea water slightly rushing on either side of our boat. Boat gently rocking as it penetrates the ocean surface. North wind touches my face. The scent of clean salt water permeates the air. We've left the past, no thought of who, where or what we do for a living.

No connecting with what we've left behind on shore and land. Just you, your boat, fellow fishermen and the Magnificent Pacific Ocean.

All of a sudden, we all hear an anxious fisherman yell, "hook up" which is our signal that he caught a first catch for the boat off a trolling line. There is a school of fish rushing by our boat. We all quickly bait our lines and cast out searching for our first catch, adrenaline racing through our bodies and exciting our lives and existence.

Then, out of long waiting moment, I feel the hit on my fishing line. Whoa, what power! What force! It pulls my line. I can hear the line being pulled out by this mighty force. I reel and reel fast, keeping my line taut, never letting up. But this fish is strong and mighty; it pulls out more and more of my line; I quickly reel in again and again, back and forth we go, this battle goes on and on. "This must be a monster," I'm thinking to myself. Muscles in my arms and shoulder crying out in pain. Then, after almost eight minutes, I finally yell "Color" which means that I have brought my fish to the surface and next to our boat. A crew hands runs to me responding to my "color" calling. He gaffs the fish and brings him up on the boat deck. What a rush? What a feeling of euphoria, my first catch!

Such was this day that I needed oh, so much.

Such a Great Feeling enjoying God's Great Gift

And three good-size Yellow Fin Tuna.

Title: To Have and To Hold
The Location – Driving in a car
The Players: me and my friend, John

Scene: My friend John and I are driving to Tio Tacos for lunch and a beer after shooting some arrows at the Riverside Archery Range. While driving I start the conversation by posing a question to John

John, we've been friends since high school, for some 60 years. I see you as an excellent friend, and a good citizen, but I've got a bone to pick with you. I really, really don't understand why you have an AR-15 along with a 30-clip magazine to hold 30 bullets.

Well Phill, Yes, we've enjoyed a long and fruitful friendship. I'll tell you why, I just love having one, such a powerful hand-held weapon that can destroy so much with one pull of the trigger, I love it.

But John why do you love it, what true satisfaction does it give you? Please explain.

That's easy. It is man-made, sleek, smooth, easy to use. You know, super user friendly.

But when in the world would you need to use it? Are you expecting a major armed invasion, or an attack by your friendly neighbors? You do know it was originally created and produced as a military assault weapon for strictly military use?

Yeah, yeah, I know. Hey, let up on me Phill, I just love it.

Ok John, aside from the military concern. Please just tell me the real reason you have one.

Alright, aright, I just like having one, a bad-ass machine, easy to use, so threating. <u>No one</u> better mess with me

Wow! What I'm hearing is you just want to be known as having what you consider a mean piece of work, and you just love the thrill of it. You not only have it, but you've shot it. How did it feel?

What can I tell you, Phill. The look of the weapon, the feel of it, the sound of it firing, it's f...g deadly. Gives me a <u>strong sense of power</u>.

Sounds like you love the thrill of it, the thrill of having it and shooting it.

You betcha. I haven't told you, Phill. I just couldn't help myself, I went out and bought a second one. It is a step up from my first one.

What, what in the world for, isn't one enough for you?

Heck no, I got one for each hand, enabling me a double the impact, two separate gun barrels, yeah, doubling the fun.

Well, John, you know I don't have one, and do not want or need one. I have a Smith & Wesson 9mm. That's enough for me.

That's a little baby gun. You need to get a real Man's gun. Come on, let's go to Turners Sporting Goods right now. I'll treat you to your first case of bullets. you'll love it.

No, no thanks, I can live without it. But, Senior John, I'll tell you what, I've got a proposition for you. I know we both like archery. We're both decent shooters on the archery target range in Riverside. I'll buy you a third AR-15 of your choice if you can outshoot me in target range contest at 50 feet. We shoot three arrows each. If you win, I'll buy you your 3rd AR-15. But if I win, you have to give me one of your two AR-15s.

No way, Phill. You're a better archery shooter than me. Nice try.

Ok John, let me sweeten the deal for you. I'll shoot from 55 feet instead of 50, giving you a clear advantage.

Boy, you are sneaky Phill, no darn way. You still got to give me more. Give me another 5 feet for a total of 60 feet from the target, and we got a deal.

Come on, chicken. I already know what my 3rd AR-15 is going to be, at $1,300 American dollars an America FN 15 Patrol 5.56 Semi-AR- 15. Yes sir Reee

In your dreams John, not going to happen, dollar limit on our bet is $325!!!

What, you tight cheapee, you're talking the lowest to the low for that type of gun

That is it take it or leave it. Here's my hand, deal?

By the way, Phillip, if you win and, I know you won't, what would you do with my gun. Have it, play with it, thrill over it, and shoot it, like me?

Heck no,

I'll tell you what I'll do with it, John. I'm pleased to inform you my newly acquired AR-15 that I will gladly and with no remorse, take from your hands and put cheerfully, into my waiting hands. Once in my possession, I will follow the recommended gun elimination procedure I'm aware of.

In my cupboard out in the garage, my soldering iron is stored. With it is a package containing an amalgam of metals that melt at a low temperature.

Phill, you lost me, what in the heck are you talking about???

With adequate materials in hand, I will proudly take my recently won AR-15 and pour molten metal into the gun barrel and seal it off with solder.

Stop, stop, you can't be serious

Thereby rendering it useless now just a pile of junk inside the recycled bin to be picked up by Waste Management this coming Monday

What, what?

To continue John, once this was "a weapon of death," will now be rendered useless and past tense. Yes sir ree, I love it, yeah.

You sorry freak, Phill. Deals off, no way

But, but, I thought we had a bet, here is my hand.

You are one sick puppy dog Phill

Ruff, ruff! I just can't help myself, I love it. I am a sick puppy dog

Ain't going to happen. Bet's off, Phill.

John, are you actually reneging, on our bet. Come on, no huevos?

You would actually do that to one of my beauties? No way, Jose.

Ok, what about I spot you another 5 feet at the archery range for a total handicap of 15 feet.

Shut up, Pendejo (Spanish for Stupid). There's our restaurant.

I'm more than ready for a beer, and a shot of strong tequila

Damn it, Phill, sometimes you really piss me off.

To have or to have not – an AR -15

The Day I'll Never Forget

This is a short story or, I guess, could be called a memoir since it describes an experience I had early in my life.

It was an overcast dreary day with a light drizzle. At the age of seven, I was in the backyard with my father on that day. I was holding tools he needed to repair a broken rain gutter that channeled rainwater from the roof to the ground below.

A man appeared at our backyard gate dressed in dark brown pants and shirt with a brown hat. He called out to my father, "Are you Mr. Sanchez?" My dad answered," Yes," and walked to the yard gate to talk to the man. The man gave my father an envelope. Then, my father walked back to me to open the envelope. Standing in the drizzle, he started to cry as he read the telegram which I thought was a letter.

He stopped working on the gutter and we both walked into the house. There in the house he gave the letter to my Uncle Bob. He too started to cry. Then, I started crying. I asked, "What's wrong, what does the letter say?" My dad said: "I'll tell you later."

The next thing I still remember, we were driving to my mom's work, at the time she was a seamstress. I still didn't know why everyone was crying. My dad went into the building and left me with my Uncle Bob. He came out with her. She was stumbling and crying so much, my Dad had to carry her. She got in the back seat with me, Then, the real tragedy began.

She was crying and yelling like she was in severe pain. She was sobbing and sobbing. She grabbed me and hugged me and just kept crying. I was really scared, and I still didn't understand why she was acting that way. For me it was really, really awful.

The next thing I remember was driving a long-long way with my mother and father. I didn't know then, but we were driving to the Clearfield City Cemetery in Clearfield, Utah.

Then, I remember being in a church sitting next to a man named Calvin. He was an uncle to Marie Sanchez, my brother's wife. I could see my parents sitting in the front row of the church. Calvin and I were about 10 – 12 rows back. In front of the church, I remember seeing a long dark wooden box lying on a table. I could not see what was in the box. There, in the church, I did see other people I did not know, crying.

Then, there were a lot of people standing outside on a lot of grass. There were a lot of men wearing the same uniform of blue, with red strips and some of them, had guns. Suddenly, gun shots were fired in the air and a horn played a somber sound which I later learned was "Taps." The official military Taps is played by a single bugle or trumpet at dusk, during flag ceremonies and at military funerals by the United Stares Armed Forces. The duration is usually around 59 seconds.

That is the memory that I carry in my heart and mind that still, to this day lingers.

Little did I know then that memory was the memory of the death of my brother, Richard Sanchez, Private, First Class, Company D, 1st Medical Battalion, 1st Marine Division. He was "killed in action" on March 3, 1952, at the age of 19 years and was posthumously awarded the Purple Heart, the Combat Action Ribbon, the Korean Service Medal, the United Nations Service Medal, and the National Defense Service Medal.

In remembering this story, I realized that this all took place when I was about 7 years old. My parents never told me my brother Richard was killed in the Korean War until I was in my early teens. I don't know what they told me about my brother missing from my life before that.

This little story explains how I did not have to go to Vietnam seventeen years later since my father appealed to the Draft Board for me. I was ready to go. But he told me, "We have already lost one son, and you are the last living son." I told him, "Dad, I still have to go and serve my country" He said, "If you go, your mother will not be able to take it, and she would probably lose the will to live."

I did not know that while all this was going on, my father had successfully appealed to the draft board. My draft status was reclassified from 1A-Available for military service, to 4A, Sole Surviving Son of the Sanchez Family. I was just 18 years old at the time, so I **did heed** my Father's request.

I really do believe that I am here but for a Father's Love of Family and, but for the Grace of God, I say these words for I truly believe I would not have survived service in the Vietnam War.

<u>So, I say now thank you to my paternal Father, Manual, and my Heavenly Father, God</u>

The Lorraine American Cemetery

Judy and I visited this Cemetery on a trip to France about 7 years ago. It was so magnificent and so well done in recognition of the American Soldiers who were killed in service to our country and freedom. Lorraine American Cemetery is located just outside the town of St. Avold, France, near the border with Germany.

It covers 113.5 acres and contains the largest number of graves of our military dead of World War II in Europe, a total of 10,481 American servicemen and women rest here.

Most were killed while driving the German forces from the fortress city of Metz, France toward the Siegfried Line and the Rhine River. Initially, there were over 16,000 Americans interred in the St. Avold region in France, mostly from the U.S. Seventh Army's Infantry and Armored Divisions and its cavalry groups. St. Avold served as a vital communications center for the vast network of enemy defenses guarding the western border of the Third Reich.

Their headstones are arranged in nine plots in a generally elliptical design extending over the beautiful rolling terrain of eastern Lorraine and culminating in a prominent overlook feature. Five are medal of Honor recipients

Inside the Memorial is a limestone memorial that rises 67 feet above the ground.
An enormous carving of St. Nabor stands high on the front memorial façade, watching over the graves.

As part of our visit, we experienced something so moving and breathtaking.

In the Cemetery there is a Sunlit Chapel. Inside, there is a beautiful altar. On the front of the altar the words in all capital letters:

"I GIVE UNTO THEM ETERNAL LIFE AND THEY SHALL NEVER PERISH"

Above the altar are magnificent Sculptures of five figures. One of the figures portrayed is George Washington.

They represent "The Eternal Struggle for Freedom."
Given our Nations recent recognition of the Battle of
Normandie in France, I write these words in respect,
recognition of those who lost their Lives in defense of
Freedom who gave "the Last Full Measure" in defense
of our beloved Nation.

AUTHOR'S BIOGRAPHY

Phillip started writing when he was in college back at the age of 19 in the late 1960s. After taking a variety of English and Literature classes at El Camino Community College, he became more involved in writing and really loved doing it. He finds expressing himself with written words on paper to be very inspirational and enjoyable. He writes in a variety of forms: poetry, stories, and critiques, many of which, are just an expose of his life.

In his academic life he obtained a Master of Science in Business Administration. He is retired now, during his working years he worked as a civilian for the United States Air Force in the field of Contracting: writing, negotiating and managing contracts. He also has enjoyed helping others through a variety of volunteer organizations. He enjoys practicing tai chi, fishing, working out and dancing.

He was able to improve his writing skills through his membership in the Moreno Valley Scribes meeting every Tuesday for about an hour and a half. The Scribes are a wonderful and friendly Writer's Group. They have made such a big difference for him in developing and fine tuning his writing skills.

"I write for the Glory of our Father, God

And For the Greater Good"

— Phillip Sanchez

Made in the USA
Monee, IL
24 March 2025